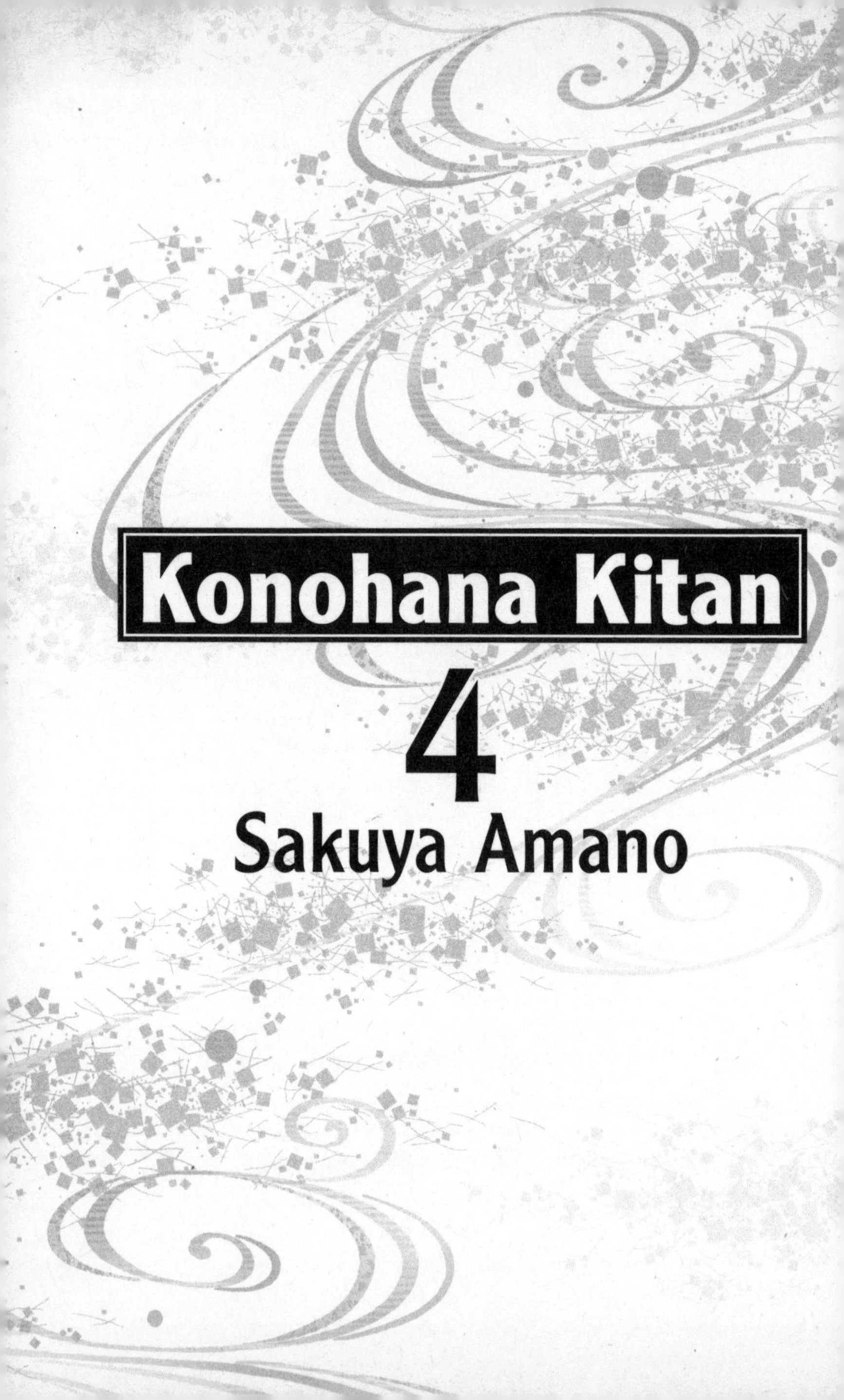
Konohana Kitan
4
Sakuya Amano

KONOHANA KITAN CONTENTS

SORRY ABOUT THIS, YUZU.
USUALLY I HAVE NATSUME CARRY MY BAGS FOR ME, BUT...
TODAY SHE'S OFF WORK.
IT'S FINE! I WAS RAISED IN THE MOUNTAINS, SO I'M USED TO HARD LABOR!
DRIP ポツ
DRIP ポツ
OH? IT'S RAINING.
I HAVE AN UMBRELLA!
NO NEED FOR THAT. WE'RE RIGHT BY ONE OF MY FAVORITE CAFÉS.
LET'S TAKE A BREAK.
Taking Shelter From the Rain

Taking Shelter From the Rain
MANGETSU
RING-A-LING

WELCOME.
OH, IF IT ISN'T KIRI-CHAN. AND YOU'VE GOT A CUTE FRIEND WITH YOU TODAY.
GASP
MY NAME IS YUZU! I WORK AT KONOHANATEI!

WHAT ARE YOU DOING, YUZU?
くすっ
CHUCKLE
TICK
カチカチ
TOCK
TICK
カチカチ
TOCK
WHAT DO YOU WANT TO DRINK?
OH, UM... I'M FINE WITH ANYTHING!
IN THAT CASE, I'LL ORDER YOU SOMETHING INTERESTING.

GRIND
GRIND
GRIND
WHAT IS THIS?
FWOOSH
IT'S A MACHINE THAT BREWS COFFEE.
BOILING THE WATER RAISES THE AIR PRESSURE INSIDE THE POT.
THERE'S A FILTER HERE SO THE GROUND COFFEE DOESN'T FALL THROUGH.
BUBBLE
ゴポ
THE BOILING WATER IS PUSHED UP THROUGH THE GLASS PIPE TO THE COFFEE BEANS.
ゴポ
BUBBLE
KLINK
KLINK
くるくる

THEN, WHEN YOU TURN OFF THE HEAT, THE AIR PRESSURE IN THE POT LOWERS—
CLICK
ボッ
WHOOSH
CLINK
コト…
GLUG
トポ
GLUG
トポ
I DON'T REALLY UNDERSTAND HOW IT ALL WORKS, BUT IT'S AMAZING!
AS LONG AS YOU UNDERSTAND THAT MUCH, IT'S FINE.
CHUCKLE

SNIFF
くんくん
IT SMELLS LIKE THE SKIN OF A BAKED SWEET POTATO!
PFFT
NO...
くすくす
GIGGLE
NO...
プル
QUIVER
NOT QUITE...
プル
QUIVER
BLOW
BLOW
ずず
SIP
OH, WHAT AN INTER-ESTING EX-PRESSION.

IS THIS SOME SORT OF BITTER MEDICINE?
I'VE HEARD IT WAS ONCE USED AS A REMEDY.
MITSUKI-CHAN, MILK AND SUGAR, PLEASE.
PLOP ポト
PLOP ポト
HOW DOES IT TASTE?
!
IT'S DELICIOUS!
GREAT.
WE'LL HAVE TWO CASTELLA CAKES, TOO.
MITSUKI-CHAN.
NOD コク

YUZU, HAVE YOU EVER TRIED CASTELLA CAKE BEFORE?
NOO...
THE CASTELLA CAKE HERE IS SPECIAL.
I'D LOVE TO TRY IT!
CHOMP CHOMP
CRUNCH CRUNCH CRUNCH
THEY USE A RATIO OF 5:3 FOR EGG YOLKS AND EGG WHITES, SO IT'S RICHER THAN REGULAR CASTELLA CAKE...
もちょもちょ
CHEW CHEW
もちょもちょ
CHEW CHEW
もちょもちょ
CHEW CHEW
もちょもちょ
CHEW CHEW
IF YOU ATE THE PAPER, YOU SHOULD SPIT IT OUT.
EMBARRASSED
ひーっ
カチャ
CLACK
AH!
THAT WAS DELICIOUS! THANK YOU VERY MUCH.

ピクピク
TWITCH
TWITCH
I SAID, "THANK YOU VERY—"
I HEARD. I HAVE GOOD EARS.
S-SORRY...
YUZU, YOU SHOULD BE QUIET IN HERE.
EVERY-ONE...
CAME HERE TO RELAX.

カチャ
CLACK

GLUG
トポトポ
GLUG

SIP
ズズズ…

KIRI-SAN, DO YOU USUALLY SIT HERE AND READ, AS WELL?
MANGETSU
HMM, NOT REALLY.
I USUALLY COME HERE WHEN I WANT TO BE ALONE.
I CAN SIT AND WATCH EVERYONE OUTSIDE.
IT'S LIKE A COMPLETELY DIFFERENT WORLD OUT THERE.

POUR
U-UM...
I MAY NOT BE MUCH HELP, BUT...

IF YOU'RE EVER WOR-RIED ABOUT SOMETHING, PLEASE TELL ME!
?
くすっ
GIGGLE
DON'T TAKE IT THE WRONG WAY!
ザァ
POUR
...
WANTING TO BE ALONE DOESN'T MAKE ME LONELY.
TAKE, FOR EXAMP-LE...
THIS COFFEE, WHICH WAS POURED JUST FOR ME...
AND THE CASTELLA, WHICH WAS PREPARED FOR ME.
THE TIME I SPEND HERE IS TIME I CAN USE FREELY.

IT'S BECAUSE I HAVE SO MANY THINGS JUST FOR "ME"...
CHOMP
THAT I CAN SHARE MY HAPPINESS WITH OTHERS!
BACK-TO-BACK BANQUETS IN THE SPRING
WE'VE BEEN SO BUSY THAT I HAVEN'T HAD THE TIME TO COME HERE.
I'M GLAD WE HAPPENED TO PASS BY!
IN THAT CASE...

MAYBE THIS SPRING SHOWER WAS MADE JUST FOR OUR SAKE TOO!
I BELIEVE IT WAS! ♪

OH, LOOK. IT STOPPED RAINING.
WE SHOULD GET BACK TO KONOHANATEI. EVERYONE'S WAITING FOR US.
カラン
RING-A-LING
U-UM...
I WAS ABLE TO RELAX AND HAVE A GREAT TIME HERE.
THANK YOU VERY MUCH.
ペコ
BOW

CHUCKLE
くすっ
DRINKING COFFEE AT A CAFÉ IS SO MUCH BETTER THAN MAKING IT YOURSELF!
HUH!? YOU REALLY MAKE IT YOURSELF AT KONOHA-NATEI?
SHALL I MAKE SOME FOR YOU NEXT TIME? I DON'T HAVE A SIPHON, THOUGH.
U-UM...
ONLY IF YOU PUT A LOT OF MILK AND SUGAR IN IT, PLEASE.

KONOHANA KITAN

Yearning for Konohanatei — Part One
SORRY FOR MAKING YOU COME ALONG ON MY ERRAND, YUZU.
I STILL OWE YOU FOR THE COFFEE, SO IT'S FINE.
SPLASH
IS THIS THE GRAVE OF ONE OF YOUR RELATIVES?
HMM, NOT TECH-NICALLY...
BUT SHE WAS LIKE FAMILY TO ME.

Yearning for Konohanatei – Part One

I'LL BE WORKING HERE STARTING TODAY. MY NAME IS KIRI.
PLEASE TEACH ME ABOUT WHAT YOU DO HERE.
KIRI'S FAMILY MEMBERS ARE KENZOKU* FOR THE DEITY DAKINI.
*KENZOKU = SERVANTS OF THE GODS; DAKINI (OR DAKINI-TEN) WAS THE INARI DEITY'S ASSISTANT
I ONLY HAVE A LITTLE BIT OF EXPERIENCE AS A KENZOKU, THOUGH.
OH, YOU HAVE A LOVELY BACK-GROUND!
PERHAPS, BUT...
I HEARD THAT KONOHANATEI HAS ALWAYS TAKEN ON KENZOKU AS ITS WORKERS.

YOU KNOW YOUR STUFF, BUT THAT'S ALL IN THE PAST.
KOZUE AND I ARE THE ONLY WORKERS LEFT WHO USED TO BE KENZOKU.
ALTHOUGH I'M A CHEF, NOT AN ATTENDANT! ♥

AND YOU'VE PUT ON THE WEIGHT TO SHOW FOR IT.
IT'S JUST PROOF THAT MY COOKING IS DELICIOUS!
UM, I'M NOT SURE IF THEY'LL SUIT YOUR PROFESSIONAL PALATE, BUT...
I BROUGHT INARI SUSHI. MY TOWN IS FAMOUS FOR IT.
OH, GOOD-NESS!

IT'S WON-DERFUL!
THANK YOU!
BOW
IF YOU'LL EXCUSE ME, I STILL HAVE TO INTRODUCE MYSELF TO THE OTHER WORKERS.

WHAT DO YOU THINK OF HER?
I THINK SHE'S A DARLING!
SHE'S ALREADY GOT YOU EATING OUT OF THE PALM OF HER HAND!
ANYWAY, WHAT I MEANT WAS...
IF SHE BELONGS TO A KENZOKU FAMILY, SHE COULD HAVE BEEN SUCCESSFUL IF SHE STAYED WITH HER FAMILY.
WOW!
I LOVE INARI!
WHY DID SHE COME TO KONOHANATEI INSTEAD?
IN THE DAYS WHEN I FIRST JOINED KONOHANATEI...

ALTHOUGH IT WASN'T PACKED TO THE MAX, IT WAS MORE LIVELY THAN IT IS NOW.
BANQUETS WERE HELD EVERY NIGHT WITH GEISHA AND JESTERS.
IT'S ONLY YOUR FIRST DAY, SO PLEASE JUST CLEAN OFF THE USED PLATES.
YES, MA'AM.
THIS HOT SAKÉ GOES TO THE AKEBONO ROOM!
OKAY!
CLATTER

GASP
I'M SO SORRY, I'LL BRING YOUR HOT SAKÉ RIGHT AWAY!

SOME OTHER GIRL ALREADY BROUGHT IT.
HUH?

THANKS FOR CLEANING UP THE KASUMI ROOM.
HUH? I DIDN'T CLEAN IT.
THEN WHO WAS IT?
EEEEK!

WHAT'S THE MATTER?
MY PEARL CLIP FELL INTO THE POND...
IT'S VERY PRECIOUS TO ME. WHAT SHOULD I DO?

キラッ
GLINT
!

THERE IT—
THERE IT IS!
SPLASH
SPLASH
W- WAIT!
YAE- CHAN?!
LOOK!

I FOUND IT, MADAM!
BATHED IN THE MOON-LIGHT...
HER WET, WHITE SKIN SHONE BRIGHTER THAN ANY PEARL.

GIVE ME A HAND, PLEASE.
SLIP
THIS WAS...
MY FATEFUL MEETING...
SPLASH
WITH YAE-SAN, THE GEISHA.

STEAMY
SORRY ABOUT THAT!
THANKS FOR LETTING ME TAKE A BATH, EVEN THOUGH I'M NOT A GUEST.
MADAM INSISTED ON IT.
GOODNESS, YOU'RE GOING TO CATCH A COLD!
HURRY AND WARM UP IN THE HOT SPRINGS!
I'LL LET OKAMI KNOW IT WAS MY ORDER.

WELL, FALLING IN THE POND WAS UNFORTUNATE...
BUT THANKS TO THAT WE GET TO ENJOY A MOONLIT BATH!
"UNFORTUNATE"? IT WAS YOUR FAULT!
WHAT'S YOUR NAME?
KIRI.
KIRI-CHAN, WHAT DID YOU DO BEFORE YOU CAME HERE?

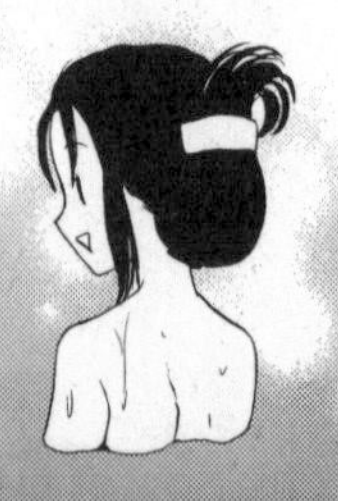

SHE SURE DOES TALK A LOT...

I WORKED WITH MY FAMILY AS A KENZOKU...
OH, I SEE!
YOU'RE DOING A GREAT JOB ASSISTING THE OTHER WORKERS, SO I SUSPECTED YOU WEREN'T JUST A NEW WORKER.
KENZOKU ARE USED TO HELPING PEOPLE, AREN'T THEY?

SHE WAS...
WATCHING ME?
YOU BROUGHT THE HOT SAKE THAT ANOTHER GIRL FORGOT, DIDN'T YOU?
I REALLY APPRECIATED THAT!

BUT WHY COME TO KONO-HANATEI?
DIDN'T YOU THINK OF FOLLOWING IN YOUR PARENTS' FOOTSTEPS AND BECOMING A KENZOKU?
IT'S NOT AN AMAZING STORY, BUT...
I HAVE A LITTLE BROTHER...
SOMEDAY, HE'LL TAKE OVER FOR MY FATHER.
EVEN IF I STAYED AT HOME, I'D JUST BE SENT AWAY ONE DAY, SO...
I DECIDED TO LEAVE AND BECOME INDEPENDENT BEFORE THAT HAPPENED.
...
YOU'RE SUCH A GOOD GIRL!

YOU'RE STILL YOUNG, BUT YOU'RE THINKING SO HARD ABOUT THE FUTURE! GOOD JOB!
SQUEEZE
チクッ
YOU'RE VERY TALENTED, KIRI-CHAN, SO I THINK YOU SHOULD DO WHAT YOU WANT TO!
GEISHAS AND WORKERS RUN IN DIFFERENT CIRCLES, BUT I HOPE WE'LL SEE EACH OTHER OFTEN! ♥
YEAH... ME TOO.

NADESHIKO, DID YOU FINISH CLEANING THE AKEBONO ROOM?
AH, NOT YET! I'LL DO IT RIGHT AWAY—
I ALREADY FINISHED CLEANING IT.

YOU ALL SEEMED BUSY, SO I TOOK CARE OF IT.
OH...
THANKS.

MIZUKI, THE HEAD ATTENDANT
KIRI? SHE'S BEEN A GREAT HELP
AND SHE'S QUICK TO LEARN.

HOWEVER, SHE'S A LITTLE...

SHE'S WHAT?
NO, IT'S NOTHING.
DON'T MIND ME.
OH, KIRI-CHAN! ♥
ARE YOU IN CHARGE OF THIS ROOM TODAY?
NO, I'M NOT IN CHARGE OF ANYTHING YET.
I'M JUST HELPING THE OTHER WORKERS.
IS THAT SO?
YOU'RE A SMART GIRL, SO I'M SURE YOU'LL HAVE YOUR OWN ROOM IN NO TIME.
LET'S BOTH WORK HARD TODAY!
くす
GIGGLE

IF I DON'T HURRY UP AND DELIVER THIS STEAMED EGG CUSTARD, IT'LL GET COLD.
THANK YOU FOR WAITING.
HERE IS YOUR STEAMED EGG CUSTARD.
BLEGH!
IT'S TOO HOT!
I'M TERRIBLY SORRY!

IT'S FINE. I JUST BURNED *MEOW* TONGUE A LITTLE.
OH, NO! AS HEAD CHEF, I CANNOT APOLOGIZE ENOUGH. PLEASE ALLOW US TO REMAKE IT, ON THE HOUSE.
THAT GUEST HAS A DELICATE TONGUE.
WE ALWAYS LET HIS STEAMED DISHES COOL BEFORE BRINGING THEM TO HIM.
DON'T FEEL TOO BAD ABOUT IT.
YOU'LL GET THE HANG OF THINGS, BIT BY BIT.
KIRI-SAN, COME HERE PLEASE!
YOU WERE THE ONE WHO CLEANED THIS ROOM, RIGHT?!
MY HAND TOWEL IS MISSING.

I PUT IT ON TOP OF THE DESK...
HUH? I THOUGHT THAT WAS A WASH RAG!
DID YOU THROW IT AWAY?!
NO, I PUT IT IN THE WASH.
I'LL GO LOOK FOR IT!
FOUND IT!
WE'RE TERRIBLY SORRY!
...
I SEE...

THIS WAS MY FAULT, AS HEAD ATTENDANT—
THAT'S NOT TRUE! IT'S BECAUSE I DID THINGS WITHOUT BEING ORDERED TO!
THAT'S RIGHT.
KIRI...
I'M SURE YOU WERE A TALENTED KENZOKU, ABLE TO COMPLETE ASSIGNMENTS ON YOUR OWN.
BUT HERE...
THE WORKERS ALL WORK AS ONE.
IF YOU MAKE A MISTAKE, EVERYONE HAS TO PAY THE PRICE FOR IT.

YOU CANNOT FORGET THAT.
...YES, MA'AM.
OH, KIRI-CHAN! ARE YOU OFF ALREADY?
GUESS WHAT? A GUEST GAVE ME CASTELLA CAKE!
LET'S SPLIT IT—

...

I SEE... SO THAT'S WHAT HAPPENED.

I FOUND OUT THAT EVERYONE WILL SUFFER IF I MAKE A MISTAKE.

I'VE BEEN WONDERING HOW TO WORK WITHOUT MAKING ANY MISTAKES...
BUT, I'M NOT SURE HOW.
HMM?!

WAIT A SECOND! DID OKAMI REALLY SAY THAT?
HUH?
SHE'S NOT TELLING YOU NOT TO MAKE MISTAKES...

SHE'S TELLING YOU TO THINK ABOUT WHY YOU MADE THE MISTAKE IN THE FIRST PLACE!
THINKING
BECAUSE I'M A NEWBIE?
MAYBE?
THAT'S NOT IT!
IT'S EASY.
YOU DON'T COMMUNICATE ENOUGH.
YOU SHOULDN'T HOLD BACK IF YOU DON'T KNOW SOMETHING. JUST ASK!
...
I'VE ALWAYS BEEN TOLD THAT I WAS NEVER A "TROUBLE CHILD."
I THOUGHT I SHOULDN'T BOTHER OTHERS, BUT...

GIGGLE
くすっ
IN THE EYES OF AN ADULT, A CHILD WHO DOESN'T CAUSE TROUBLE...
IS JUST A CHILD WHO ACTED CONVENIENTLY FOR THAT ADULT.
YOU CAME TO KONOHANATEI BECAUSE YOU WANTED TO BECOME INDEPENDENT, RIGHT?
YOU'RE NOT A CHILD ANYMORE.
THERE'S NO NEED FOR YOU TO CATER TO ADULTS' MOODS AND WHIMS.
I'M SO LUCKY THAT KIRI DOESN'T CAUSE TROUBLE.

SHE ALWAYS BEHAVES WELL...
SO I HAVE MORE TIME AND FREEDOM TO LOOK AFTER HER LITTLE BROTHER.
SUPPORT YOUR BROTHER ONCE HE'S OLDER, OKAY?
ACTUALLY...
I LIED WHEN I SAID I WANTED TO BE INDEPENDENT.
ALL I REALLY WANTED WAS TO GET OUT OF THAT HOUSE.

NOW I KNOW...
I MADE THOSE MISTAKES BECAUSE I WASN'T COMPLETELY DEVOTED TO MY WORK.
AH...I HATE THIS!
I'M NOT TALENTED OR GREAT OR ANYTHING!
I DIDN'T MEAN TO COMPLAIN LIKE THIS!

YOU MUST HAVE HAD A HARD TIME...
ALL BY YOURSELF, UNTIL NOW.

わあああああ…
WAAAIL
YAE-SAN HELD ME...
AND STROKED MY HAIR THE ENTIRE TIME I CRIED.
I WAS EMBARASSED THAT I COULDN'T STOP CRYING, AND AFTER I APOLOGIZED...
YOU KNOW...
ADDING A LITTLE BIT OF SALT BRINGS OUT THE SWEETNESS EVEN MORE.
くすっ
GIGGLE
SHE SAID THAT, AND STROKED MY HEAD AGAIN.

BA-DUMP
ドキ
BA-DUMP
ドキ
"IT'S EASY."
"YOU DON'T COMMUNICATE ENOUGH."
U-UM, NADESHIKO-SAN...
COULD YOU PLEASE TEACH ME HOW TO WARM UP THE SAKÉ?
?!
HUH? *ME?*
IT'S FINE IF YOU'RE BUSY...
OH, I'M NOT BUSY!
I JUST THOUGHT YOU'D NEVER ASK ME FOR SOMETHING LIKE THAT.
...HUH?

AFTER ALL, YOU HAD THE JOB DOWN PAT RIGHT FROM THE START.
I'VE ACTUALLY FELT LIKE YOU'VE BEEN THE ONE HELPING *ME* OUT!
SOMETIMES I GET EM-BARRASSED WHILE TEACHING OTHERS, BUT...
YOU CAN ASK ME ANYTHING!
SO THAT'S WHAT SHE THINKS OF ME...
I GOT THE IMPRESSION THAT YOU DIDN'T LIKE TO BE FUSSED OVER.
I THOUGHT IT WAS BETTER TO LET YOU DO THINGS YOUR WAY INSTEAD OF PUSHING OUR WAY ONTO YOU.
THEY WERE ALL BEING CON-SIDERATE OF ME...
I THOUGHT I WAS DOING MY JOB ALONE...
BUT THEY WERE WATCHING OVER ME THE ENTIRE TIME.
"HERE, THE WORKERS ALL WORK AS ONE."

OKAMI-SAN!
UM...
I'M TERRIBLY SORRY ABOUT YESTERDAY!
I'LL DO MY BEST NOT TO MAKE MISTAKES OR CAUSE TROUBLE FOR EVERYONE!
BLOW
WHO DO YOU WORK FOR?
UM... FOR KONOHANA-TEI?
NOPE.
F-FOR YOU?!
NO!

GEISHAS AND ATTENDEES, ALL OF US WORK FOR THE SAKE OF OUR GUESTS!
AS LONG AS YOU'RE WORKING FOR THEM, IT'S FINE IF YOU CAUSE US A LITTLE TROUBLE...
BECAUSE WE'RE ALL FAMILY HERE.
"YOU MUST HAVE HAD A HARD TIME ALL BY YOURSELF, UNTIL NOW."

TH-THANK YOU VERY MUCH!
I'M NOT...
ALONE ANYMORE.
KIRI-CHAN!

HELLO, YAE-SAN!
COULD YOU BABYSIT THIS GIRL FOR A LITTLE WHILE?
"THIS GIRL"...?
MY MOTHER USUALLY LOOKS AFTER HER, BUT SHE HAD TO GO OUT TODAY.
THIS IS MY DAUGHTER, SAKURA.
HER FATHER ISN'T IN THE PICTURE, THOUGH.
THANKS A BUNCH!

THAT WAS HOW I MET A YOUNG SAKURA.
I DIDN'T KNOW SHE WAS A MOTHER...
HOW-EVER...
THAT'S A STORY FOR ANOTHER TIME.

KONOHANA KITAN

Destiny

きゃわ
SQUEAL
きゃわ
SQUEAL
KU-CHAN STOLE MY TOY!
WHERE'S MOMMY?
SORRY. THEY'RE SO LOUD.
I'M HUNGRY!

WHAT'S ALL THIS?! WHEN DID KONOHANATEI BECOME A DAY CARE?
APPARENTLY THEY'RE RELATED TO ONE OF OUR GUESTS.
WHY ARE THERE SO MANY?!
HEY, I GOTTA GO PEE-PEE!
EEK
THAT LADY'S GOT CRAZY EYES!
BWAAA!
SHOCK
WHAT DID SHE SAY?!
PLEASE DON'T MAKE THEM CRY.
IT'S NOT MY FAULT!
SAKURA! DON'T HANG OUT WITH THESE KIDS!
I CAN'T TELL YOU APART FROM THEM!
FLOP
FLOP
IT'S A FISHY!

HEY, YUZU IS GOOD WITH KIDS!
WHERE'S SHE AT?!
YUNTAN IS HELPING KIRI-SAN RIGHT NOW.
YOU SHOULDN'T RELY ON HER SO MUCH, Y'KNOW.
I DON'T RELY ON HER THAT MUCH!

GRIMACE
HURRY UP AND LET ME GO HOME.
I'VE GOT CATS AT HOME THAT ARE PROBABLY STARVING.
AS I SAID, YOU'VE ALREADY PASSED AWAY.
THERE MAY BE A PATH TO THE HEAVENS, BUT THERE ISN'T ONE BACK TO EARTH.
HUH? I'VE NEVER HEARD THAT!
THAT'S WHAT MOST PEOPLE SAY.

WHO'S GOING TO TAKE CARE OF MY CATS NOW THAT I'M GONE?
THERE'S NO NEED TO WORRY ABOUT THAT.
AS SPECIFIED IN YOUR WILL, THEY'LL RECEIVE AN INHERITANCE AND BE SENT TO CAT SANCTUARIES.
YOUR NEIGHBOR, SHIROU-KUN, WILL TAKE CARE OF THEM UNTIL THEN.
SHIROU-CHAN WILL? I SEE...
AT LEAST I KNOW THEY'LL BE IN GOOD HANDS.
NOW I HAVE NO LINGERING ATTACHMENTS TO THIS WORLD.

GAAAH
PITTER
PATTER
KYA
HA
HA
WHAT'S GOING ON? IT SURE IS NOISY.
I'M SORRY, IT MUST BE THE PEOPLE IN THE OTHER BANQUET HALL.
OFTEN, FRIENDS AND FAMILY OF THOSE WHO HAVE PASSED AWAY HAVE A WELCOME PARTY TO GREET THEM.
IT SURE TOOK YOU LONG ENOUGH!
YOUR LEFT HAND SHOWED UP BEFORE YOU DID!
ONE FAMOUS MANGA WRITER WAS GREETED BY A GROUP OF YŌKAI*.
HA HA! A WELCOME PARTY?
EVEN THOUGH THEIR LIVING FRIENDS ARE STILL MOURNING THEIR DEATHS? ISN'T THAT STRANGE?
HA
HA
HA
NOT THAT I HAVE ANYONE MOURNING ME.
TCH

ŌKAI = SUPERNATURAL BEINGS FROM JAPANESE FOLKLORE

IT MAY BE RUDE TO ASK THIS, BUT WHAT ABOUT YOUR FAMILY?
MY FAMILY MEMBERS ARE ALL FOOLISH AND MY "FRIENDS" ARE DETESTABLE.
THEY LOATHED ME AND CALLED ME NEKOMATA.*

*THE NEKOMATA IS A FELINE YŌKAI THAT KILLS AND EATS PEOPLE, BUT THIS IS ALSO A PLAY ON HER NAME, KATSUMATA.

THEN YOU MUST HAVE A LOT OF CAT FRIENDS!
HMPH! I DIDN'T CARE FOR THEM BECAUSE I LIKE THEM, YOU KNOW.

IT STARTED WHEN I PICKED UP SOME KITTENS THAT HAD BEEN ABANDONED IN THE PARK.
MEOW
MEOW

FIVE NEWBORN KITTENS WHO STILL HAD THE UMBILICAL CORDS ATTACHED...
THEY HAD BEEN PLACED IN A PLASTIC BAG AND TOSSED ASIDE.
SMALL ENOUGH TO BE MISTAKEN FOR RATS.
MEOW MEOW
MEOW
CAN YOU SAVE THEM?
XO VETERINARIAN
I WAS TIRED AFTER GETTING OFF WORK,
BUT I HAD TO FEED THEM EVERY THREE HOURS...
KITTENS CAN'T PEE OR POOP ON THEIR OWN, SO YOU HAVE TO STIMULATE THEM WITH A WET COTTON BALL.
PEE...
I PROBABLY WANTED TO SAVE THEM SO MUCH...
BECAUSE I FELT OBLIGATED TO...
TWO LITTLE BABIES PASSED AWAY...
SHIRO BIT SOMEONE...
SO WE NEED TO PUT HIM DOWN.

WHEN I WAS YOUNGER, I COULDN'T SAVE MY PET DOG.
I WASN'T AIMING FOR ATONEMENT...
BECAUSE I WAS SICK OF FEELING LIKE I NEEDED IT.

BUT DESTINY IS A FUNNY THING.
I DIDN'T WALK AROUND LOOKING FOR ABANDONED KITTENS...
MEOW
MEOW
MEOW
SPLASH
BUT I ALWAYS SEEMED TO FIND THEM.

THEY KEPT MULTIPLYING UNTIL MY HOUSE WAS OVERFLOWING WITH CATS.
HA HA!
THE FACT THAT YOU DIDN'T THROW THEM OUT OF YOUR HOUSE SHOWS HOW SINCERE YOU ARE, NEKOMATA-SAMA!
THAT ISN'T MY NAME, YOU KNOW.
I'M SURE THE CATS WHO MET YOU WERE ALL VERY HAPPY.
...
I WONDER ABOUT THAT.

THERE WERE SOME CATS WHO DIED THE DAY I PICKED THEM UP.
I WONDER IF I CAN REALLY SAY THAT I SAVED THEM...
KU-CHAN...
KU-CHAN, I'M SO SORRY.
SORRY...
FOR EVERY KITTEN I PICKED UP AND SAVED...
THERE WAS ANOTHER CAT IN A CITY FAR AWAY THAT DIED WITHOUT ANYONE FINDING IT.
WHAT IF MY ACTIONS WERE SOME SORT OF EUGENOCIDE?
THAT THOUGHT CONTINUES TO PLAGUE ME, EVEN AFTER MY DEATH.

I DON'T KNOW HOW IT FEELS TO BE A SAVIOR...
BUT I *DO* KNOW HOW IT FEELS TO BE SAVED.
...
RIGHT NOW, I'M ALIVE BECAUSE A HUMAN PICKED ME UP.
SHE FOUND ME FROZEN UNDER A PILE OF SNOW.
IF THAT WAS DESTINY, AS YOU SAY IT MIGHT BE...
THEN I AM GRATEFUL FOR THAT DESTINY.

MEOW
MEOW
MEOW
I'M THANKFUL THAT SHE...
NOTICED MY PITIFUL CRIES...
AND ANSWERED MY FAINT PLEAS FOR HELP.
"BUT I ALWAYS SEEMED TO FIND THEM."

バタバタバタ
TAP
TAP
TAP
HEY, YOU CAN'T JUST BARGE IN THERE!
MOMMY!
MOMMY, MOMMY!
HURRY UP! WE'VE BEEN WAITING SO LONG!
WE'VE ALL BEEN WAITING FOR YOU!

ARE THEY...?
IT SEEMS YOUR FAMILY HAS COME TO GREET YOU!
ALTHOUGH SOME OF THEM HAVE ALREADY BEEN REBORN AND LEFT THIS WORLD.
MOMMY, MOMMY! LISTEN!
GIMME YOUR HAND!
I CAN SEE NOW!
AND IT DOESN'T HURT TO BREATHE!
IS THAT SO? HOW WONDER-FUL.
THANK YOU FOR COMING TO SEE ME, KU-CHAN.
YOU GAVE ME A NAME, SO I DIDN'T GET LOST!
A NAME?

A NAME IS PROOF THAT YOU EXISTED.
BECAUSE YOU GAVE NAMES EVEN TO THE KITTENS WHO DIED SOON AFTER YOU FOUND THEM...
THEY WERE ABLE TO RETURN TO YOU WITHOUT LOSING THEIR WAY.

GRANNY...
IT'S TIME TO GO UP THERE, NOW.
IF IT ISN'T SHIROU-CHAN, FROM NEXT DOOR!
WHAT ARE YOU DOING, DYING SO YOUNG? YOUR POOR PARENTS MUST BE HEART-BROKEN!
I'M STILL ALIVE, REALLY!
I HAVE TO GO BACK NOW...
SO THIS IS GOODBYE.

WHY DIDN'T YOU TELL HER?
HMM...
ピョコ
POP
WELL, I'M NOT A DOG ANYMORE.

I'LL HAVE TO KEEP IT A SECRET, UNTIL I GO UP THERE TO SEE HER.
くすくす
GIGGLE
MOURNING
MOURNING
SPIRIT LANTERNS
SPIRIT LANTERNS
GRANNY KATSUMATA PASSED AWAY?
SHE LIVED ALONE AND DIDN'T HAVE ANY FAMILY, SO I HEARD THE BOY NEXT DOOR FOUND HER.
OH, HOW AWFUL...
SPIRIT LANTERNS
SHE MUST HAVE LED A LONELY LIFE.
PURR
ごろごろ
PURR
BUT LOOK...

DOESN'T
SHE LOOK
PEACEFUL?

KONOHANA KITAN

A Summer Night's Dream
URINOSUKE
A YOUNG BOAR DEMON NAMED BAKU THAT HATCHED OUT OF AN EGG SAKURA FOUND. HIS FAVORITE FOOD IS NIGHTMARES. EVERYONE AT KONOHANATEI THINKS HE'S A WILD BOAR PIGLET.

ずび…
SLIDE
OH, URINOSUKE, DID YOU CATCH A SUMMER COLD?
SNEEZE
SPRING ONIONS ARE GOOD FOR CURING COLDS.
SPRING ONIONS? YOU MEAN TO WRAP AROUND YOUR NECK?
I THOUGHT YOU'RE SUPPOSED TO STICK THEM UP YOUR BUTT?
GINGER IS GOOD, TOO.
ESPECIALLY IF YOU BOIL IT WITH ALCOHOL, SUGAR, SOY SAUCE, AND MIRIN.
KIRI
ああっ
YAWN
AGH, I WANT TO EAT BOAR STEW!
SHIVER

FWAP
ALL DONE!
AMAZING!
WOW! WHAT IS THIS THING?
IT'S A MOSQUITO NET, TO KEEP THE BUGS AWAY WHILE WE'RE SLEEPING.
HEY, GET OFF OF THERE!
WE ONLY HAVE ONE, SO WE'LL HAVE TO PACK IN LIKE SARDINES UNDER IT.

NACCHAN, DON'T STEAL THE BLANKET!
ALL RIGHT EVERYONE, GOOD NIGHT.
GOOD NIGHT!
SNEEZE

IT SURE IS CRAMPED...
SATSUKI, HAVE YOU GOTTEN FATTER?
SHUT UP!
THIS IS MY FIRST TIME SLEEPING LIKE A SARDINE! ♥
モワ WAFT
モワ WAFT
SLIDE...
UGH...
UGH...
SUCK

ふぇ
PHEW
SNEEZE
WAFT
モワ
WAFT
モワ
SPLASH
MMPH...
URGH...
SLIME
モワ
WAFT
モワ
WAFT
モワ
WAFT
WAFT
SNEEZE
SNEEZE

...
THIS IS...
A DREAM.
YOU KNOW THOSE REALLY REALISTIC PEOPLE WHO SHOW UP IN YOUR DREAMS?
WHO ARE YOU?
SPARKLE SPARKLE
NO ONE SUSPICIOUS, I CAN SAY THAT MUCH.
I JUST GOT LOST!

I AM THE SPIRIT OF DREAMS, KYRIELL—
SWOOSH
YOU LOOK JUST LIKE SOMEONE I KNOW, SO I REACTED WITHOUT THINKING...
I DON'T THINK THAT'S A GOOD ENOUGH EXCUSE TO TRY AND PUNCH ME, BUT FINE.
THIS IS MY DREAM, ISN'T IT?!
GET THAT ANNOYING FACE OUT OF HERE!
ACTUALLY, THIS ISN'T YOUR DREAM.
HUH? WHAT DO YOU MEAN?
FIRST OF ALL, DREAMS CAN BE BROKEN INTO TWO MAJOR CATEGORIES.

THE FIRST IS "DREAMS CREATED BY BRAINS."
THESE ARE DREAMS YOU CREATE BASED ON YOUR REAL-LIFE WORRIES AND DESIRES.
WHEN YOU FEEL DRIVEN INTO A CORNER IN REAL LIFE, YOU RUN AWAY IN A SUBCONSCIOUS NIGHTMARE.
WHEN YOU'RE IN A RE-LAXED AND DEEP SLEEP.
DEADLINE
WHEN YOU'RE NERVOUS AND CAN'T SLEEP WELL.
THE SECOND TYPE IS "DREAMS SEEN BY YOUR SOUL."
THESE OCCUR WHEN YOUR SOUL TRAVELS TO THE WORLD ABOVE AND VIEWS THE SCENERY THERE.
IN THAT WORLD, YOU CAN EVEN MEET WITH THE DECEASED OR PEOPLE WHO ARE FAR AWAY FROM YOU.
PROPHETIC DREAMS ALSO FALL INTO THIS CATEGORY.

THE DREAM WE'RE IN NOW IS ONE MADE BY YOUR BRAIN.
WHAT IS SHE TALKING ABOUT?
WE'RE STILL INSIDE YOUR HEAD, SO OTHERS SHOULDN'T BE ABLE TO ENTER.
HOWEVER, *SOMETHING* HAS AFFECTED THIS AND CAUSED MANY DREAMS TO OVERLAP. I CAN'T RETURN TO MY OWN DREAM, EITHER.
WE NEED A HERO...
THOSE PUPPY EYES WON'T WORK. I KNOW YOU'RE TRYING TO PUSH THIS OFF ON ME—
SEND ME BACK TO MY DREAM. IF YOU DON'T, I'LL BE STUCK INSIDE YOUR HEAD FOREVER...
I THOUGHT YOU WEREN'T AN EVIL SPIRIT?!

TWEET
TWEET!
WHISTLE
WHERE ARE WE?
THIS SEEMS LIKE THE DREAM OF A FEMININE YOUNG LADY.
TROT
TROT
SHAKE
NOW I KNOW WHOSE DREAM WE'RE IN.

THAT'S...!
WHAT A BEAUTIFUL PRINCESS!
I'LL TAKE HER BACK TO THE CASTLE AND MAKE HER MY WIFE...

ドキドキ
BA-DUMP
BA-DUMP
ドキ
BA-DUMP
チラ
PEEK
いやああっ
SHRIEK
THE DWARVES ARE MULTI-PLYING!
REN, YOU'VE NEVER READ THE ORIGINAL SNOW WHITE STORY, HAVE YOU?

IN IT, THE PRINCESS COUGHS UP THE POISONOUS APPLE FROM THE IMPACT OF HER COFFIN BEING DROPPED.
HOW COULD THE PRINCE MAKE YOU THROW UP WITH A KISS? HE MUST HAVE REALLY BAD BREATH...
YOU'VE ALREADY TRAMPLED ALL OVER MY DREAM, I DON'T NEED A LECTURE TO TOP IT ALL OFF!
TWEET
ANYWAY, HAVE YOU SEEN ANYONE ELSE?
THAT'S JUST A FAKE YOU WISHED UP.
WHAT'S SO WRONG WITH THAT? I CAN MAKE ANYTHING A REALITY IF I BELIEVE IN IT!
IT CAN BE REAL FOR ME!
RAGE
THAT'S PURE ESCAPISM.

HEY REN, EVERY-ONE!
I JUST MET A NICE OLD LADY WHO GAVE ME SOME APPLES!
LET'S EAT THEM TOGETHER!
FWUMP
SEE? ISN'T THAT THE BEST WAY TO GET SOMEONE TO CHOKE SOMETHING UP?
HMM?
THESE ARE...

MASS-PRODUCED DOLLS THAT HAVE BEEN LOVED BY GIRLS FOR GENERA-TIONS!
ROAR
I HATE EVERY DETESTABLE TOY THAT STOLE MY PLACE AS THE MOST CHERISHED DOLL!
OKIKU?!
SHE'S EATING THEM?!
THIS IS BAD... SHE'S GONE INTO A BLIND RAGE AND FORGOTTEN ABOUT US!
LET'S GET OUT OF HERE!

GASP
CRAP! THIS IS...
THE PHENOMENON OF RUNNING AT FULL SPEED AND STILL GETTING NOWHERE THAT OFTEN APPEARS IN DREAMS!
SLIP
I FEEL YOUR PAIN!
SLIP
SLIP
CUT IT OUT, OKIKU!
HAVEN'T YOU HAD ENOUGH REVENGE? THAT'S ALL IN THE PAST!
FROM NOW ON, WE'LL PLAY WITH YOU A LOT!
...REN?
I'VE BEEN SO HAPPY... SINCE I MET YOU GUYS...
THAT'S RIGHT! SO STOP THIS AND—
BUT...!

I HATE THE IDEA THAT THOSE DOLLS MAY BE HAPPY, TOO!
I LIKE HOW YOU ALWAYS LAY THINGS OUT STRAIGHT.
YOU'RE RIGHT, THAT'S A DIFFERENT PROBLEM.
SAKURA'S OVER THERE!
...WHAT?
SAKURA, YOU CAN'T COME OVER HERE NOW, IT'S TOO DAN-GEROUS!
TA-DA!
WAIT, YOU'RE GOING TO FIGHT TOO?!

コォォォ…
ROAR
WOW
COOL!
BY THE WAY, WHERE'S YUZU?
OH, HER?
SHE'S PROBABLY FAST ASLEEP.
HUH?
ONCE SHE FALLS ASLEEP SHE SLEEPS LIKE THE DEAD, SO SHE SAID SHE RARELY EVER HAS DREAMS.
WAKE UP!
USUALLY DOESN'T SLEEP WELL
AH, SO THAT'S WHY SHE'S NOT HERE.

AT THAT TIME, YUZU WAS...
OH? WHAT'S THIS?
THIS IS THE PLACE I SOMETIMES SEE IN MY DREAMS...
BUT I ALWAYS FORGET ABOUT IT WHEN I WAKE UP!
プギー
SNUFFLE
OH, URINOSUKE, YOU'RE HERE TOO?

HE'S OUR PET WILD BOAR. THANK YOU FOR TAKING CARE OF HIM.
HUH?
GASP
SATSUKI-CHAN?!
OH NO, SHE NEEDS MY HELP!
U-UM, I WONDER WHAT I CAN DO TO SAVE HER...

カァァァ
HISS
EEK
ジャキーン
SNIP
ドスーン
KA-THUNK
I DON'T WANT TO PLAY HAIR-DRESSER!
TEE-HEE! ♡
DON'T COME THIS WAY!
ドスーン
KA-THUNK

THERE, THERE.
WAIL
BWAH
IF WE STICK AROUND, SAKURA WILL MAKE US INTO HER TOYS. LET'S RUN AWAY SOMEWHERE...
HMM?
WHAT IS THAT? DOES IT LEAD ALL THE WAY TO HEAVEN?
JUST LIKE IN "THE SPIDER'S THREAD" BY AKUTAGAWA!
OKAY, ALL WE HAVE TO DO IS CLIMB THIS AND—
WHAM

THIS IS MY THREAD, EVERYBODY ELSE BACK OFF!
*RED CARD
YOU REALLY NEED TO READ MORE!
DON'T FALL, SATSUKI!
CRAP...
WHY AM I GETTING SO TIRED EVEN THOUGH IT'S JUST A DREAM?
PANT
PANT

SNAP
...!
YUZU!
I'M HERE!

I CAME TO SAVE YOU, SATSUKI-CHAN!
PANT
PANT
YUZU...?

ARE YOU THE REAL YUZU?
YES!
BUT YOU SAID YOU NEVER HAVE DREAMS...
I USUALLY FORGET THEM RIGHT AFTER WAKING UP, SO I JUST NEVER NOTICED...
I'LL PROBABLY FORGET THIS DREAM, TOO.
I'M JUST GLAD I COULD SAVE YOU.
YEAH, THANKS TO THAT SPIDER'S THREAD...
ずび…
SLIDE
GROSS!

EWWW, I CAN'T BELIEVE I TOUCHED THAT!
I THOUGHT IT WAS A LITTLE STICKY...
WHERE DID YOU APPEAR FROM, ANYWAY?
OH, UM...
SATSUKI-CHAN CALLED MY NAME, SO...
"YUZU!"

THIS IS THE WORLD OF "DREAMS VIEWED BY YOUR SOUL."
SO AS LONG AS YOUR FEELINGS ARE RECIPROCATED, YOU CAN MEET WITH SOMEONE EVEN ON THE OTHER SIDE OF THE WORLD!
HUH? THAT WASN'T KIRI-SAN?
BY THE WAY, IN THE PAST, JAPANESE PEOPLE DIDN'T THINK THEIR CRUSHES APPEARED IN THEIR DREAMS BECAUSE THEY LIKED THAT PERSON...
SHE'S SO ATTRACTED TO ME, SHE APPEARED IN MY DREAM!
THEY BELIEVED IT WAS THE OTHER WAY AROUND. SCARY, ISN'T IT?
IS THAT TRUE, SATSUKI-CHAN?
HUH...?
I LOVE YOU TOO, SO THAT MAKES ME REALLY HAPPY!
NO, WAIT, JUST CALM DOWN A SECOND!
YOU SHOULDN'T SAY SOMETHING LIKE THAT SO LIGHTLY...
CUT IT OUT!
WHISTLE
WHISTLE

IT'S JUST A DREAM, SO YOU SHOULD OPENLY ADMIT YOUR FEELINGS FOR ONCE!
I HOPE YOU TWO ARE HAPPY TOGETHER!
N-NO...
ST-STOP!
WAH!
IF THIS IS A DREAM, LET ME WAKE UP!
GASP
CHIRP
CHIRP

HUFF
IT'S MORNING ...
MMPH...
FWAP
LOVE YOU... SATSUKI-CHAN...
MUMBLE
PFFT.
TOO BAD SHE'LL FORGET ONCE SHE WAKES UP...
WELL...

I GUESS IT WASN'T THAT BAD OF A DREAM.

ALTHOUGH IT COULD HAVE ENDED SOONER.

EPILOGUE
SNUFFLE
NOW YOU HAVE A STOM-ACHACHE, URINOSUKE?
IT LOOKS LIKE HE OVERATE, BUT ON WHAT?
THE REST OF THE NIGHTMARES EVERYONE LEFT BEHIND.

KONOHANA KITAN

"WILL YOU DRAW A BODY FOR ME?"
A PAIR OF GHOSTLY LEGS ASKED THIS OF ME...

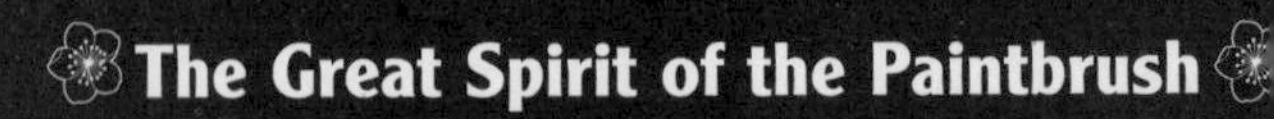

The Great Spirit of the Paintbrush

KREE
KREE
WHAT IS THIS PLACE...?
I THOUGHT I WAS ON AN OVERNIGHT BUS...
WHY AM I IN THE MIDDLE OF A FOREST?
FLASH
AH!
A LIGHT! SOMEONE MUST BE OVER THERE!
IS ANYONE THERE?!

WELCOME TO
KONOHANATEI!

HELLO, GREAT SPIRIT!
...HUH?
WAH!
Y-YOU'VE GOT IT ALL WRONG! I'M NOT A GUEST HERE!
I JUST GOT LOST...!
NO, YOU'RE A GREAT SPIRIT.
EEK
A FURRY?!

THAT THING YOU'RE HOLDING IN YOUR RIGHT HAND...
A PIECE OF WOOD?
WHAT IS THIS? WHEN DID IT APPEAR?
IT'S YOUR GUEST PASS.
IT'S PROOF THAT YOU'RE ALLOWED TO STAY HERE AT KONOHANATEI.
PLEASE FORGET ABOUT YOUR REALITY AND ENJOY YOURSELF.
TOSS
ポイッ
MY NAME IS YUZU, AND I'LL BE TAKING CARE OF YOU DURING YOUR STAY HERE! ♥
WHAT IS THIS PLACE, A ZOO RIP-OFF?
IF THEY'RE NOT WEARING FURRY SUITS, THEY'RE WEARING CAT EARS...

THERE MUST BE A MISTAKE!
I WAS JUST GOING HOME ON AN OVERNIGHT BUS AND...!
WHAT IS THIS "BUS" YOU SPEAK OF?
UM, IT'S LIKE A BIG CAR...
IS IT LIKE A CARRIAGE?
AM I SO FAR IN THE COUNTRYSIDE THAT THEY DON'T EVEN HAVE BUSES?!
?
!

LET'S SEE...
IT WOULD BE FASTER TO DRAW A PICTURE THAN TRY AND EXPLAIN...
A BUS IS A RECTANGULAR CAR, LIKE THIS.
IT DOESN'T HAVE HORSES BECAUSE IT BURNS FUEL...
POP

OH, YOU'RE RIGHT! IT'S MOVING WITHOUT HORSES!
WOW!
VROOM

JERK
IT CRASHED ITSELF?!
SHOCK
THE THINGS YOU DRAW COME TO LIFE? THAT'S AMAZING!
SPARKLE
SPARKLE
HUH?! NO, THAT'S NOT...!
YOU'RE THE GREAT SPIRIT OF THE PAINTBRUSH, AREN'T YOU?

IT'S ALWAYS BEEN MY DREAM TO MAKE A LIVING FROM MY ART.

WHEN I LIVED IN THE COUNTRY, EVERYONE TREATED ME LIKE A GOD BECAUSE MY ART WAS SO GOOD.

I BELIEVED THAT I WAS TALENTED.

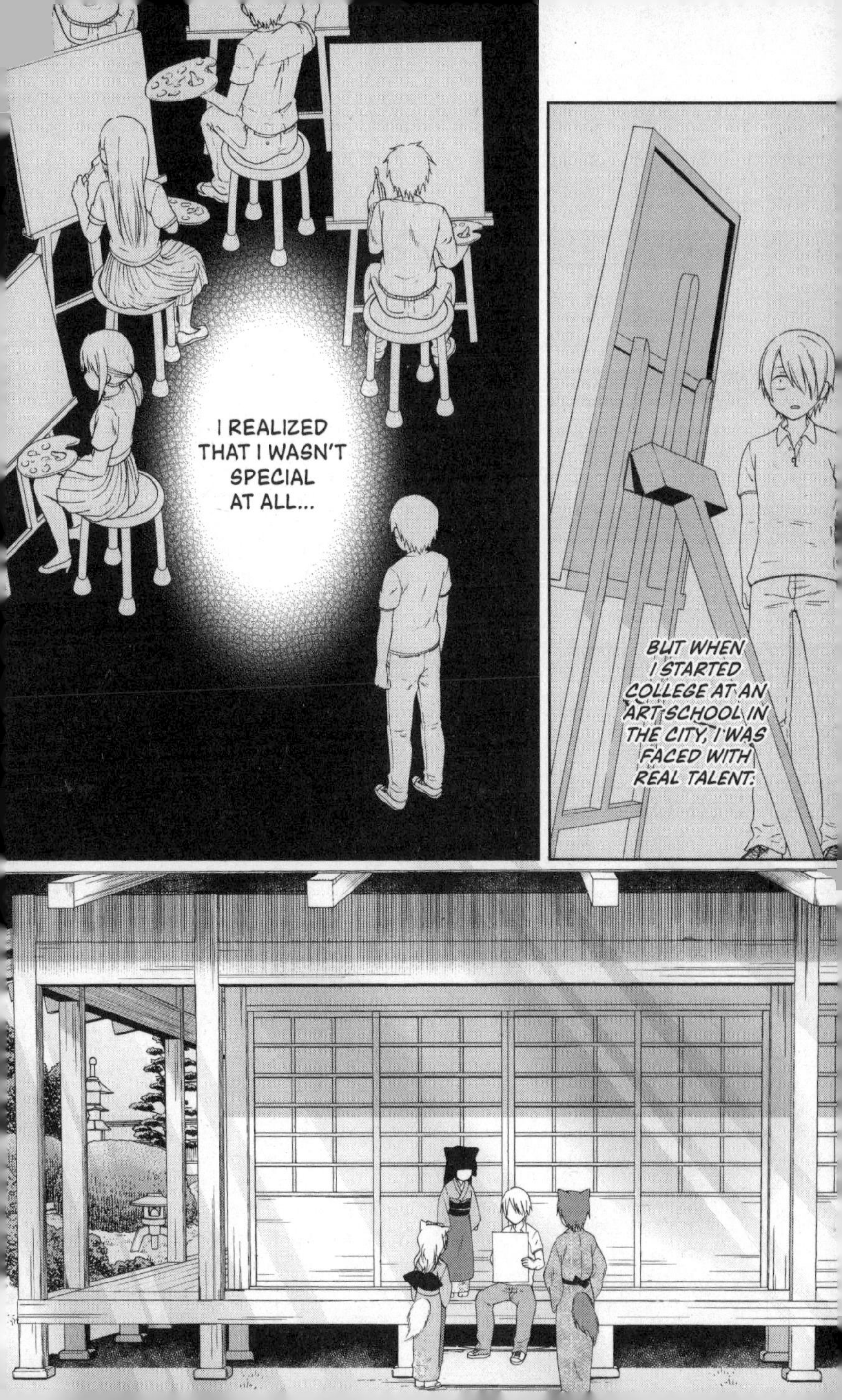
BUT WHEN I STARTED COLLEGE AT AN ART SCHOOL IN THE CITY, I WAS FACED WITH REAL TALENT.
I REALIZED THAT I WASN'T SPECIAL AT ALL...

WOW! YOUR DRAWING REALLY CAME TO LIFE!
C-COULD YOU PLEASE DRAW SOMETHING FOR ME, TOO?
SURE. WHAT DO YOU WANT?
I WANT CINDERELLA'S PUMPKIN CARRIAGE!
THAT'S A FAIRY TALE, ISN'T IT? NOT EVEN A GOD CAN DRAW SOMETHING HE'S NEVER SEEN IN REAL LIFE.
SKRITCH
SKRITCH
HOW'S THIS?
SQUEAL
THANK YOU SO, SO MUCH!
BUT I CAN'T RIDE IN THIS!
SHOCK
I CAN ONLY DRAW SOMETHING AS BIG AS THE PAPER WILL ALLOW...

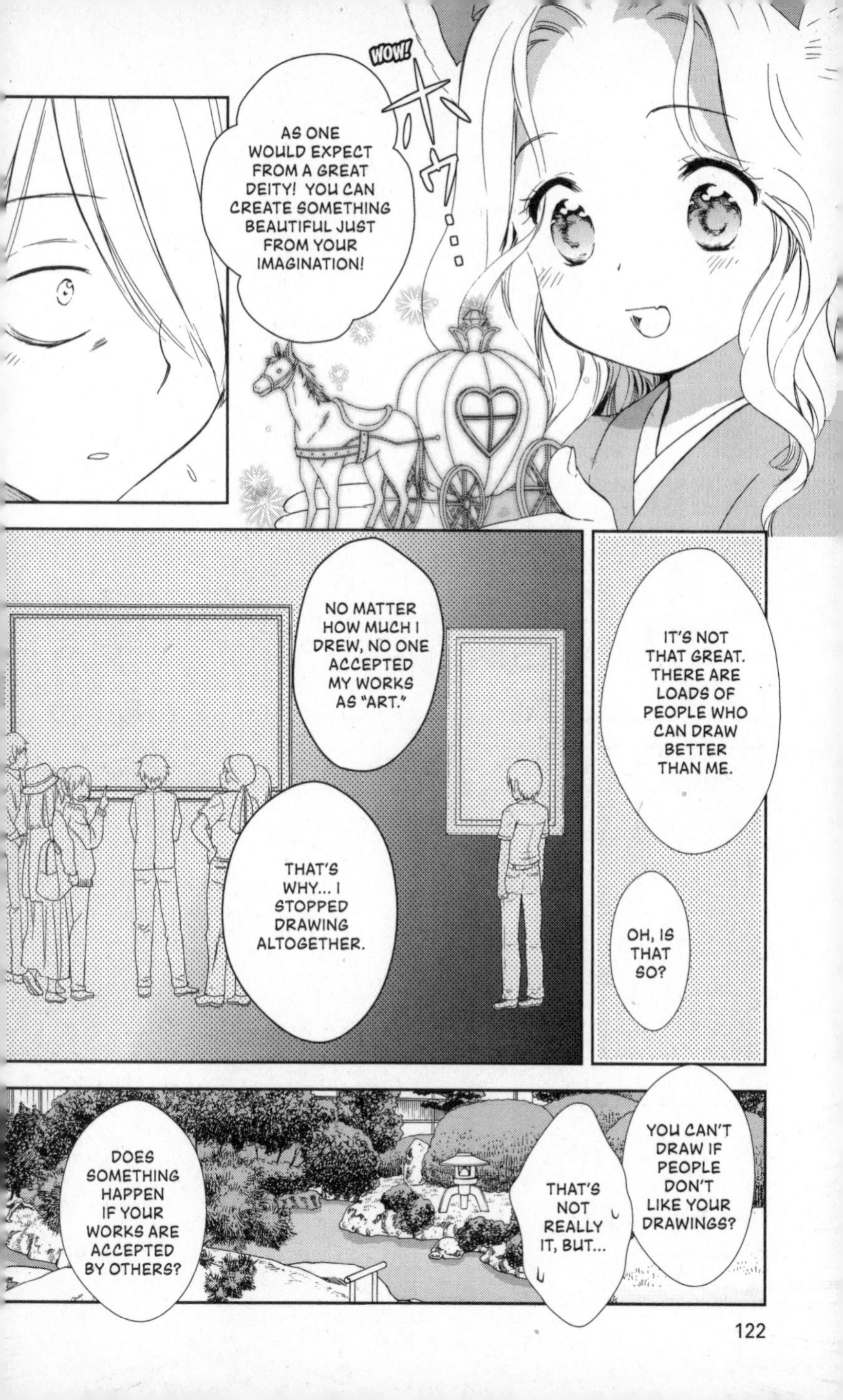
WOW!
AS ONE WOULD EXPECT FROM A GREAT DEITY! YOU CAN CREATE SOMETHING BEAUTIFUL JUST FROM YOUR IMAGINATION!
IT'S NOT THAT GREAT. THERE ARE LOADS OF PEOPLE WHO CAN DRAW BETTER THAN ME.
OH, IS THAT SO?
NO MATTER HOW MUCH I DREW, NO ONE ACCEPTED MY WORKS AS "ART."
THAT'S WHY... I STOPPED DRAWING ALTOGETHER.
YOU CAN'T DRAW IF PEOPLE DON'T LIKE YOUR DRAWINGS?
THAT'S NOT REALLY IT, BUT...
DOES SOMETHING HAPPEN IF YOUR WORKS ARE ACCEPTED BY OTHERS?

UM... THEY GIVE YOU MONEY... AND STUFF.
YOU BECOME FAMOUS AND ARE CALLED A MASTER...
HA HA HA
YOU WANT TO BE CALLED "MASTER" EVEN THOUGH YOU'RE ALREADY A DIVINE SPIRIT? THAT'S SO WEIRD!
GREAT SPIRIT...
COULD YOU PLEASE DRAW SOMETHING FOR THIS YOUNG MAN?
SURE. WHAT SHOULD I DRAW?
A BOAT! I WANT A BOAT!
SKRITCH
SKRITCH
FLAP
FLAP
WOAH, THAT'S SO COOL!

THANKS!
NOW I CAN GO TO MY MAMA AND PAPA!

HE SAID HE LOST SIGHT OF HIS PARENTS DURING A BOATING ACCIDENT.

I'M SLOWLY STARTING TO REALIZE...

HE'S AT PEACE...
THANKS TO YOU, GREAT SPIRIT.

...ME?
YES!
BECAUSE YOU DREW THAT BOAT FOR HIM!

YOUR ART SAVED HIM.

THAT THIS MAY NOT BE THE REAL WORLD.

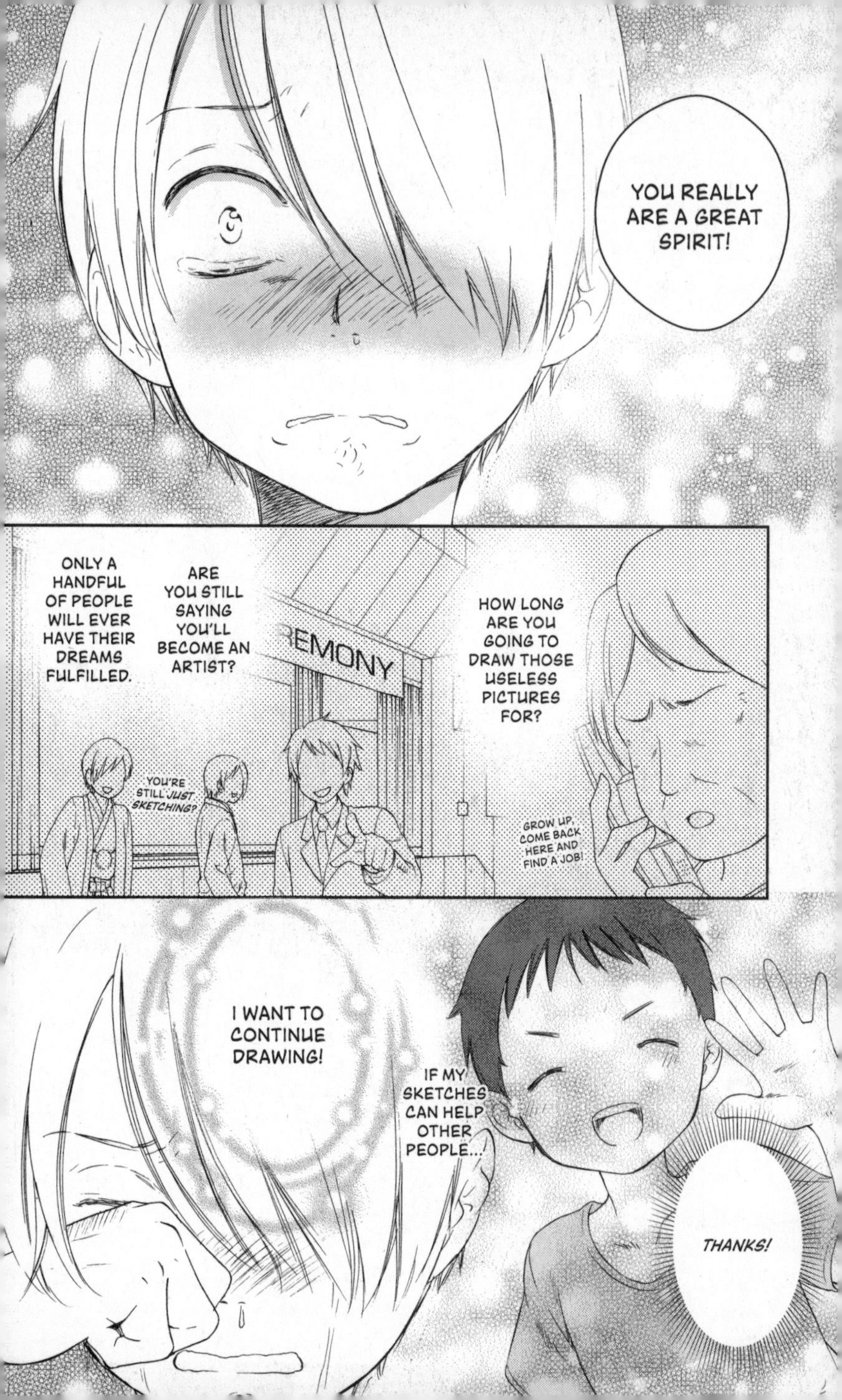
YOU REALLY ARE A GREAT SPIRIT!
HOW LONG ARE YOU GOING TO DRAW THOSE USELESS PICTURES FOR?
GROW UP, COME BACK HERE AND FIND A JOB!
REMONY
ARE YOU STILL SAYING YOU'LL BECOME AN ARTIST?
ONLY A HANDFUL OF PEOPLE WILL EVER HAVE THEIR DREAMS FULFILLED.
YOU'RE STILL *JUST* SKETCHING?
THANKS!
IF MY SKETCHES CAN HELP OTHER PEOPLE...
I WANT TO CONTINUE DRAWING!

GREAT SPIRIT, WHY ARE YOU CRYING?
ヒ PITTER
タ PATTER
ヒ PITTER
タ PATTER
ヒ PITTER
タ PATTER
GREAT SPIRIT, PLEASE DRAW A SWING FOR ME!
HA HA HA
YAY!

GREAT SPIRIT, WHY DON'T YOU TAKE A BREAK?
REQUESTS ARE MADE FOR YOUR DRAWINGS EVERY DAY...
I'M FINE. I'M JUST GLAD THAT MY SKETCHES ARE BEING ENJOYED.
I HAVEN'T DRAWN ANYTHING FOR YOU YET, HAVE I?
DO YOU HAVE A REQUEST? I CAN DRAW ANYTHING.
I HAVE NO NEED FOR A DRAWING.
YOU DON'T HAVE JUST HOLD BACK! JUST ASK!
I'M NOT HOLDING BACK...

THERE ARE OTHER DEITIES THAT CAN MAKE DRAWINGS COME TO LIFE.
IT'S NOT THAT RARE OF A TALENT.
DIDN'T KNOW THAT.
...HUH?
S-SAT-SUKI-CHAN!
THAT WAS SO RUDE OF YOU!
WHY? IT'S WORSE TO PRETEND I'M INTERESTED, ISN'T IT?
SATSUKI-CHAN!
EVEN NOW, I'M STILL NOT...
SPECIAL AT ALL.

IN THIS DAY AND AGE, PLENTY OF CHILDREN CAN DRAW AT THIS LEVEL.
THERE'S NOTHING PARTICULARLY SPECIAL ABOUT YOUR DRAWINGS.
BA-DUMP

SNAP
...
GREAT... SPIRIT?

...I CAN'T DRAW ANYTHING.
EVEN THOUGH I WAS BLESSED WITH THIS NEW POWER...
THEY EVEN REFERRED TO ME AS A DEITY...
IN THE END... I WASN'T OFFERING ANYTHING THEY HADN'T SEEN BEFORE.
"THERE ARE OTHER DEITIES THAT CAN MAKE DRAWINGS COME TO LIFE."
UN-BELIEV-ABLE!
PLEASE...

DRAW ME
A BODY.
?!

GAAH
WH-WHAT IS THIS? A GHOST THAT ONLY HAS LEGS?!
USUALLY IT'S THE OTHER WAY AROUND, ISN'T IT?!
PLEASE...
I DON'T HAVE A BODY, SO I WAS TOLD I CAN'T GO TO HEAVEN.
SO PLEASE, DRAW ME ONE.
SAVE ME, LIKE YOU SAVED THAT BOY.
"NOW I CAN GO TO MY MAMA AND PAPA!"

...
I...
CAN SAVE YOU?
GREAT SPIRIT...
I'VE BROUGHT YOUR DINNER.
YOU CAN JUST LEAVE IT THERE!
I'M IN THE MIDDLE OF A MAJOR WORK NOW, SO PLEASE DON'T INTERRUPT ME.
UNDER-STOOD.

THIS IS HARD...
I'VE NEVER DRAWN A CHILD BEFORE.
I'M 4 FEET AND 3 INCHES TALL, AND I WEIGH...
I HAVE TO CREATE A COMPLETE IMAGE JUST FROM THE DESCRIPTIONS SHE TELLS ME...
BUT...
POP

WOW, THIS IS AMAZING! I CAN MOVE MY ARMS AND LEGS!
THERE'S NOTHING MORE SATIS-FYING...
THANK YOU!
THAN MY DRAWING OF HER COMING TO LIFE.
NO, THANK *YOU!*
THIS IS THE MOST FUN I'VE EVER HAD DRAWING!
YOUR COMPLETED BODY...
WILL PROBABLY BECOME MY GREATEST MASTER-PIECE!

I'VE ALWAYS WANTED TO ENJOY MY ART THIS MUCH...
TIME TO TAKE A BREAK...
EXCUSE ME.
YOUR STAY HERE WILL END TOMORROW.
PLEASE DECIDE WHERE YOU WILL JOURNEY TO AFTERWARDS.
WHAT DO YOU MEAN BY "WHERE"?
WILL YOU GO TO HEAVEN...
OR BACK TO THE HUMAN WORLD?

WAIT, I'M NOT DEAD YET?
I THOUGHT THIS WAS HEAVEN.
YOU'RE RIGHT ON THE BRINK!
I SEE...
I CAN STILL CHOOSE WHERE TO GO...
MY LAST MEMORY BEFORE COMING HERE...
IS OF A SHATTERING IMPACT...
A THUNDEROUS ROAR...
AND PANICKED VOICES.

THE OVERNIGHT BUS I WAS RIDING PROBABLY HAD AN ACCIDENT...
ZZZ
I DIDN'T EVEN THINK ABOUT WHAT HAPPENED TO MY MATERIAL BODY...
MY LIFE HASN'T AMOUNTED TO MUCH, AFTER ALL.

HA HA!
EVEN IF I WENT HOME, I'D JUST GO BACK TO BEING USELESS.
I'D RATHER USE THE POWER...
IN MY RIGHT HAND TO HELP OTHERS.
IS THAT SO?
BUT YOU KNOW...
I'LL GO TO HEAVEN.

A PERSON'S WORTH ISN'T DEPENDENT ON WHETHER OR NOT THEY WERE HELPFUL.
THAT'S THE WORTH OF A TOOL.
THAT BLONDE WORKER SAID SOME NICE THINGS...
BUT I HAVE NO LINGERING ATTACHMENTS TO THAT WORLD.
HER WORDS HAD NO EFFECT ON ME.
ONCE I DRAW YOUR FACE, YOU'LL BE FINISHED!
WOW, THIS IS SO COOL!
POP
YOU'RE LIKE A WIZARD!
"YOU'RE JUST LIKE A WIZARD!"
I'VE HEARD THOSE WORDS BEFORE...

JUST THE OTHER DAY, IN FACT...
I'VE ALWAYS WANTED A DRESS LIKE THIS!
BUT I WAS TOO EMBARRASSED TO WEAR ONE, SO I ALWAYS WORE SHORTS AND A SWEATSHIRT.
YOU'RE...
THAT GIRL?

THE GIRL WHO SAT NEXT TO ME ON THE OVERNIGHT BUS?
YOU'RE DRAWING? WHAT IS IT? SHOW ME!
WOW, THESE ARE AMAZING!
HEY, CAN YOU DRAW A CAT?
THEY LOOK SO REAL! YOU CAN DRAW ANYTHING, CAN'T YOU?
YOU'RE JUST LIKE A WIZARD!
WHY...
WHY ARE YOU A GHOST NOW?!

I DON'T HAVE A BODY, SO I CAN'T GO TO HEAVEN.
THE FACT THAT SHE DOESN'T HAVE A BODY HERE...
GASP
MEANS THAT SHE'S STILL ALIVE!
PLEASE DRAW ME A BODY!
IT HURTS... PLEASE SAVE ME!
GREAT SPIRIT...
RATTLE
カラ...
IT'S TIME FOR YOU TO DEPART ON YOUR JOURNEY.

WAIT...
WAIT A MINUTE! I HAVE TO HELP HER, FIRST!
DO NOT WORRY.
SHE WILL FOLLOW YOU TO HEAVEN SHORTLY.
EVERYTHING YOU DRAW WITH YOUR RIGHT HAND...
BELONGS TO HEAVEN, AFTER ALL.
DO YOU SWEAR?

YOU'LL REALLY DRAW A PICTURE OF ME?
BUT I'M NOT GOOD AT PORTRAITS...
I REALLY LOVE YOUR DRAWINGS!
HEY...
I CAN STILL CHOOSE, RIGHT?
TO GO TO HEAVEN...
OR BACK TO EARTH?

YES. THE DECISION IS YOURS, GREAT SPIRIT.
GRAB
SPLASH

MY BODY IS DISAP-PEARING!
WHY WOULD YOU... DO THAT...?
ARE YOU SURE ABOUT THIS?
DON'T YOU WANT TO BE A DEITY?

DESPITE THAT...
I'M NOT A DEITY.
NOR AM I AN ARTIST OR A WIZARD.
THAT GIRL WAS KIND ENOUGH...
TO SAY THAT SHE LOVED MY ART...
FINE.
WHEN WE GET OFF THE BUS TOMORROW, I'LL DRAW YOUR PICTURE.
I'M GOING HOME.
I MADE A PROMISE WITH HER...

THANK YOU FOR STAYING WITH US, VALUED GUEST...
POUR
MUTTER
MUTTER
OW...
RUSTLE

ヒュ
HUFF
ヒュ
HUFF
HEY, IS ANYBODY THERE?

IT WAS PROBABLY JUST SOME FALLING ROCKS.
W- WAIT...
WE'RE... HERE...
SOMEONE, PLEASE...

WE'RE HERE!
WE'RE STILL HERE!
PLEASE...
POUR
WE'RE STILL ALIVE!
CLATTER
CLATTER

AH, NOW I GET IT...
I WASN'T THE ONE WHO BECAME A GOD...
IT WAS MY RIGHT HAND.

BY THE WAY, I WONDER WHAT HAPPENED TO THAT ONE GUEST.
YES.
I WONDER IF HE'S DOING ALL RIGHT.
WELL, IF HE'S NOT FINE, I'M SURE HE'LL FIND HIS WAY BACK HERE.
HA HA HA! THAT'S RIGHT!
I GUESS THAT MEANS...
THAT HE'S ALIVE, SOMEWHERE DOWN THERE.

KNOCK
コン
KNOCK
コン
COME IN.
YOU REALLY ARE HERE!
GUESS WHAT? TODAY THEY TESTED MY LEGS...
AND SAID THAT IF THEY HEAL RIGHT, I'LL BE ABLE TO WALK AGAIN!
THAT'S GREAT!
AH, ARE YOU DRAWING AGAIN?

I HAVE TO USE MY LEFT HAND NOW, SO IT'S NOT THAT GREAT...
THAT'S NOT TRUE! IT'S REALLY NICE!
I PROMISE I'LL DRAW YOU...
ONCE I GET USED TO DRAWING WITH THIS HAND, OKAY?
OKAY!
WHOSE HOUSE IS THIS?
IT'S SO PRETTY! I WISH I COULD VISIT THERE!
HE-HE...
WHY ARE YOU LAUGH-ING?

Konohana Kitan #4 - The End

KONOHANA KITAN

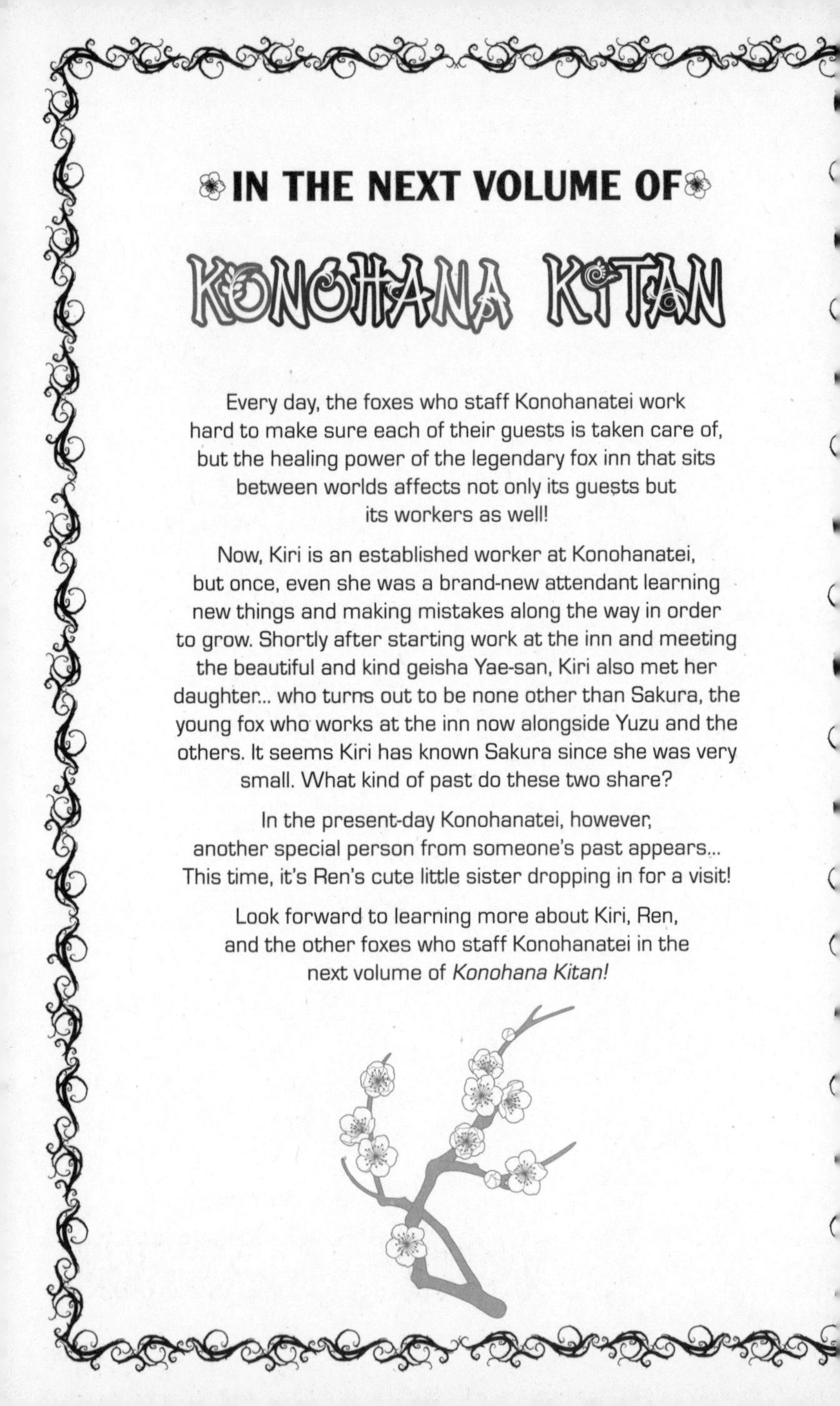

IN THE NEXT VOLUME OF

KONOHANA KITAN

Every day, the foxes who staff Konohanatei work hard to make sure each of their guests is taken care of, but the healing power of the legendary fox inn that sits between worlds affects not only its guests but its workers as well!

Now, Kiri is an established worker at Konohanatei, but once, even she was a brand-new attendant learning new things and making mistakes along the way in order to grow. Shortly after starting work at the inn and meeting the beautiful and kind geisha Yae-san, Kiri also met her daughter... who turns out to be none other than Sakura, the young fox who works at the inn now alongside Yuzu and the others. It seems Kiri has known Sakura since she was very small. What kind of past do these two share?

In the present-day Konohanatei, however, another special person from someone's past appears... This time, it's Ren's cute little sister dropping in for a visit!

Look forward to learning more about Kiri, Ren, and the other foxes who staff Konohanatei in the next volume of *Konohana Kitan!*

Futaribeya

A ROOM FOR TWO

It's Sakurako Kawawa's first day of high school, and the day she meets her new roommate – the incredibly gorgeous Kasumi Yamabuki!

Follow the heartwarming, hilarious daily life of two high school roommates in this new, four-panel-style comic!

ARIA The MASTERPIECE

☆ DELUXE, REMASTERED 2-IN-1 EDITION
☆ GORGEOUS GOLD-FOIL COVER
☆ INCLUDES FULL-COLOR ILLUSTRATIONS

The Grimm's Tales reimagined in manga!

Beautiful art by the talented Kei Ishiyama!

Stories from Little Red Riding Hood to Hansel and Gretel!

TOKYOPOP
• PRESENTS •

UNDEAD
MESSIAH
KAMO
PACT WITH THE SPIRIT WORLD

Ocean
of
Secrets

Sword Princess
Amaltea
Natalia Batista
GOLDFISCH

TOKYO
POP

Secret INSPECTOR!
READ FOR FREE ON
POP COMICS®
AVAILABLE ON
ANDROID APP ON Google play
Download on the App Store
Bloodivores
时空囚徒
Bloodivores © Tencent Comics - Created by Bai Xiao / Secret Inspector © 2016 by Byeongcheol KIM & Changho SON

Konohana Kitan Volume 4

Sakuya Amano

Editor	-	Lena Atanassova
Marketing Associate	-	Kae Winters
Technology and Digital Media Assistant	-	Phillip Hong
Translator	-	Katie McLendon
Copy Editors	-	Massiel Gutierrez & Zac Romick
QC	-	Risa Otsuka
Graphic Designer	-	Phillip Hong
Retouching and Lettering	-	Vibrraant Publishing Studio
Editor-in-Chief & Publisher	-	Stu Levy

A  Manga

TOKYOPOP Inc.
5200 W. Century Blvd. Suite 705
Los Angeles, 90045

E-mail: info@TOKYOPOP.com
Come visit us online at www.TOKYOPOP.com

www.facebook.com/TOKYOPOP
www.twitter.com/TOKYOPOP
www.pinterest.com/TOKYOPOP
www.instagram.com/TOKYOPOP

ISBN: 978-1-4278-5978-5

First TOKYOPOP Printing: April 2019

10 9 8 7 6 5 4 3 2 1

Printed in CANADA

STO

THIS IS THE BACK OF THE BOOK!

How do you read manga-style? It's simple! To learn, just start in the top right panel and follow the numbers: